★ WELCOME BABY ★

GUESTS

NAME AND RELATIONSHIP TO PARENTS

ADVICE FOR PARENTS

WISHES FOR BABY

GUESTS

NAME AND RELATIONSHIP TO PARENTS

ADVICE FOR PARENTS

WISHES FOR BABY

GUESTS

NAME AND RELATIONSHIP TO PARENTS

ADVICE FOR PARENTS

WISHES FOR BABY

GUESTS

NAME AND RELATIONSHIP TO PARENTS

ADVICE FOR PARENTS

WISHES FOR BABY

GUESTS

NAME AND RELATIONSHIP TO PARENTS

ADVICE FOR PARENTS

WISHES FOR BABY

GUESTS

NAME AND RELATIONSHIP TO PARENTS

ADVICE FOR PARENTS

WISHES FOR BABY

GUESTS

NAME AND RELATIONSHIP TO PARENTS

ADVICE FOR PARENTS

WISHES FOR BABY

GUESTS

NAME AND RELATIONSHIP TO PARENTS

ADVICE FOR PARENTS

WISHES FOR BABY

GUESTS

NAME AND RELATIONSHIP TO PARENTS

ADVICE FOR PARENTS

WISHES FOR BABY

GUESTS

NAME AND RELATIONSHIP TO PARENTS

ADVICE FOR PARENTS

WISHES FOR BABY

GUESTS

NAME AND RELATIONSHIP TO PARENTS

ADVICE FOR PARENTS

WISHES FOR BABY

GUESTS

NAME AND RELATIONSHIP TO PARENTS

ADVICE FOR PARENTS

WISHES FOR BABY

GUESTS

NAME AND RELATIONSHIP TO PARENTS

ADVICE FOR PARENTS

WISHES FOR BABY

GUESTS

NAME AND RELATIONSHIP TO PARENTS

ADVICE FOR PARENTS

WISHES FOR BABY

GUESTS

NAME AND RELATIONSHIP TO PARENTS

ADVICE FOR PARENTS

WISHES FOR BABY

GUESTS

NAME AND RELATIONSHIP TO PARENTS

ADVICE FOR PARENTS

WISHES FOR BABY

GUESTS

NAME AND RELATIONSHIP TO PARENTS

ADVICE FOR PARENTS

WISHES FOR BABY

GUESTS

NAME AND RELATIONSHIP TO PARENTS

ADVICE FOR PARENTS

WISHES FOR BABY

GUESTS

NAME AND RELATIONSHIP TO PARENTS

ADVICE FOR PARENTS

WISHES FOR BABY

GUESTS

NAME AND RELATIONSHIP TO PARENTS

ADVICE FOR PARENTS

WISHES FOR BABY

GUESTS

NAME AND RELATIONSHIP TO PARENTS

ADVICE FOR PARENTS

WISHES FOR BABY

GUESTS

NAME AND RELATIONSHIP TO PARENTS

ADVICE FOR PARENTS

WISHES FOR BABY

GUESTS

NAME AND RELATIONSHIP TO PARENTS

ADVICE FOR PARENTS

WISHES FOR BABY

GUESTS

NAME AND RELATIONSHIP TO PARENTS

ADVICE FOR PARENTS

WISHES FOR BABY

GUESTS

NAME AND RELATIONSHIP TO PARENTS

ADVICE FOR PARENTS

WISHES FOR BABY

GUESTS

NAME AND RELATIONSHIP TO PARENTS

ADVICE FOR PARENTS

WISHES FOR BABY

GUESTS

NAME AND RELATIONSHIP TO PARENTS

ADVICE FOR PARENTS

WISHES FOR BABY

GUESTS

NAME AND RELATIONSHIP TO PARENTS

ADVICE FOR PARENTS

WISHES FOR BABY

GUESTS

NAME AND RELATIONSHIP TO PARENTS

ADVICE FOR PARENTS

WISHES FOR BABY

GUESTS

NAME AND RELATIONSHIP TO PARENTS

ADVICE FOR PARENTS

WISHES FOR BABY

GUESTS

NAME AND RELATIONSHIP TO PARENTS

ADVICE FOR PARENTS

WISHES FOR BABY

GUESTS

NAME AND RELATIONSHIP TO PARENTS

ADVICE FOR PARENTS

WISHES FOR BABY

GUESTS

NAME AND RELATIONSHIP TO PARENTS

ADVICE FOR PARENTS

WISHES FOR BABY

GUESTS

NAME AND RELATIONSHIP TO PARENTS

ADVICE FOR PARENTS

WISHES FOR BABY

GUESTS

NAME AND RELATIONSHIP TO PARENTS

ADVICE FOR PARENTS

WISHES FOR BABY

GUESTS

NAME AND RELATIONSHIP TO PARENTS

ADVICE FOR PARENTS

WISHES FOR BABY

GUESTS

NAME AND RELATIONSHIP TO PARENTS

ADVICE FOR PARENTS

WISHES FOR BABY

GUESTS

NAME AND RELATIONSHIP TO PARENTS

ADVICE FOR PARENTS

WISHES FOR BABY

GUESTS

NAME AND RELATIONSHIP TO PARENTS

ADVICE FOR PARENTS

WISHES FOR BABY

GUESTS

NAME AND RELATIONSHIP TO PARENTS

ADVICE FOR PARENTS

WISHES FOR BABY

GUESTS

NAME AND RELATIONSHIP TO PARENTS

ADVICE FOR PARENTS

WISHES FOR BABY

GUESTS

NAME AND RELATIONSHIP TO PARENTS

ADVICE FOR PARENTS

WISHES FOR BABY

GUESTS

NAME AND RELATIONSHIP TO PARENTS

ADVICE FOR PARENTS

WISHES FOR BABY

GUESTS

NAME AND RELATIONSHIP TO PARENTS

ADVICE FOR PARENTS

WISHES FOR BABY

GUESTS

NAME AND RELATIONSHIP TO PARENTS

ADVICE FOR PARENTS

WISHES FOR BABY

GUESTS

NAME AND RELATIONSHIP TO PARENTS

ADVICE FOR PARENTS

WISHES FOR BABY

GUESTS

NAME AND RELATIONSHIP TO PARENTS

ADVICE FOR PARENTS

WISHES FOR BABY

GUESTS

NAME AND RELATIONSHIP TO PARENTS

ADVICE FOR PARENTS

WISHES FOR BABY

GUESTS

NAME AND RELATIONSHIP TO PARENTS

ADVICE FOR PARENTS

WISHES FOR BABY

GUESTS

NAME AND RELATIONSHIP TO PARENTS

ADVICE FOR PARENTS

WISHES FOR BABY

GUESTS

NAME AND RELATIONSHIP TO PARENTS

ADVICE FOR PARENTS

WISHES FOR BABY

GUESTS

NAME AND RELATIONSHIP TO PARENTS

ADVICE FOR PARENTS

WISHES FOR BABY

GUESTS

NAME AND RELATIONSHIP TO PARENTS

ADVICE FOR PARENTS

WISHES FOR BABY

GUESTS

NAME AND RELATIONSHIP TO PARENTS

ADVICE FOR PARENTS

WISHES FOR BABY

GUESTS

NAME AND RELATIONSHIP TO PARENTS

ADVICE FOR PARENTS

WISHES FOR BABY

GUESTS

NAME AND RELATIONSHIP TO PARENTS

ADVICE FOR PARENTS

WISHES FOR BABY

GUESTS

NAME AND RELATIONSHIP TO PARENTS

ADVICE FOR PARENTS

WISHES FOR BABY

GUESTS

NAME AND RELATIONSHIP TO PARENTS

ADVICE FOR PARENTS

WISHES FOR BABY

GUESTS

NAME AND RELATIONSHIP TO PARENTS

ADVICE FOR PARENTS

WISHES FOR BABY

GUESTS

NAME AND RELATIONSHIP TO PARENTS

ADVICE FOR PARENTS

WISHES FOR BABY

GUESTS

NAME AND RELATIONSHIP TO PARENTS

ADVICE FOR PARENTS

WISHES FOR BABY

GUESTS

NAME AND RELATIONSHIP TO PARENTS

ADVICE FOR PARENTS

WISHES FOR BABY

GUESTS

NAME AND RELATIONSHIP TO PARENTS

ADVICE FOR PARENTS

WISHES FOR BABY

GUESTS

NAME AND RELATIONSHIP TO PARENTS

ADVICE FOR PARENTS

WISHES FOR BABY

GUESTS

NAME AND RELATIONSHIP TO PARENTS

ADVICE FOR PARENTS

WISHES FOR BABY

GUESTS

NAME AND RELATIONSHIP TO PARENTS

ADVICE FOR PARENTS

WISHES FOR BABY

GUESTS

NAME AND RELATIONSHIP TO PARENTS

ADVICE FOR PARENTS

WISHES FOR BABY

GUESTS

NAME AND RELATIONSHIP TO PARENTS

ADVICE FOR PARENTS

WISHES FOR BABY

GUESTS

NAME AND RELATIONSHIP TO PARENTS

ADVICE FOR PARENTS

WISHES FOR BABY

GUESTS

NAME AND RELATIONSHIP TO PARENTS

ADVICE FOR PARENTS

WISHES FOR BABY

GUESTS

NAME AND RELATIONSHIP TO PARENTS

ADVICE FOR PARENTS

WISHES FOR BABY

GUESTS

NAME AND RELATIONSHIP TO PARENTS

ADVICE FOR PARENTS

WISHES FOR BABY

GUESTS

NAME AND RELATIONSHIP TO PARENTS

ADVICE FOR PARENTS

WISHES FOR BABY

GUESTS

NAME AND RELATIONSHIP TO PARENTS

ADVICE FOR PARENTS

WISHES FOR BABY

GUESTS

NAME AND RELATIONSHIP TO PARENTS

ADVICE FOR PARENTS

WISHES FOR BABY

GUESTS

NAME AND RELATIONSHIP TO PARENTS

ADVICE FOR PARENTS

WISHES FOR BABY

GUESTS

NAME AND RELATIONSHIP TO PARENTS

ADVICE FOR PARENTS

WISHES FOR BABY

GUESTS

NAME AND RELATIONSHIP TO PARENTS

ADVICE FOR PARENTS

WISHES FOR BABY

GUESTS

NAME AND RELATIONSHIP TO PARENTS

ADVICE FOR PARENTS

WISHES FOR BABY

GUESTS

NAME AND RELATIONSHIP TO PARENTS

ADVICE FOR PARENTS

WISHES FOR BABY

GUESTS

NAME AND RELATIONSHIP TO PARENTS

ADVICE FOR PARENTS

WISHES FOR BABY

GUESTS

NAME AND RELATIONSHIP TO PARENTS

ADVICE FOR PARENTS

WISHES FOR BABY

GUESTS

NAME AND RELATIONSHIP TO PARENTS

ADVICE FOR PARENTS

WISHES FOR BABY

GUESTS

NAME AND RELATIONSHIP TO PARENTS

ADVICE FOR PARENTS

WISHES FOR BABY

GUESTS

NAME AND RELATIONSHIP TO PARENTS

ADVICE FOR PARENTS

WISHES FOR BABY

GUESTS

NAME AND RELATIONSHIP TO PARENTS

ADVICE FOR PARENTS

WISHES FOR BABY

Attach Keepsakes and Pictures

⋆ GIFT LOG ⋆

★ GIFT LOG ★

GIFT RECEIVED	GIVEN BY

★ GIFT LOG ★

GIFT RECEIVED	GIVEN BY

★ GIFT LOG ★

GIFT RECEIVED	GIVEN BY

★ GIFT LOG ★

GIFT RECEIVED	GIVEN BY

★ GIFT LOG ★

GIFT RECEIVED	GIVEN BY

★ GIFT LOG ★

GIFT RECEIVED	GIVEN BY

★ GIFT LOG ★

GIFT RECEIVED	GIVEN BY

★ GIFT LOG ★

GIFT RECEIVED	GIVEN BY

★ GIFT LOG ★

GIFT RECEIVED	GIVEN BY

★ GIFT LOG ★

GIFT RECEIVED	GIVEN BY

Made in the USA
Monee, IL
17 July 2023

39407704R00065